20

other reasons to kiss a frog

frog

LWS
BOOKS
©2006

Also from Jonathan Richard Cring

FICTION:
I'M . . . the legend of the son of man
Liary
Mr. Kringle's Tales . . . 26 stories 'til Christmas
Holy Peace

NONFICTION:
Jesonian
Finding the Lily (to consider)
Digging for Gold (in the rule)
Preparing a Place (for myself)
20 Other Reasons to Kiss a Frog
Living a Legendary Life

SCREENPLAYS:
Hank's Place
Lenders Morgan

The Man with the Red Hat (short)
Baptism 666
Gobel
Iz and Pal
Newer
Inside (short)
12/23 (short)

MUSICAL COMPOSITIONS:
I'M . . . a Jesonian serenade
Cloud of Witnesses (a requiem of renewal)
Have yourself a Clazzy Little Christmas
To Everything a Season – Ingathering/Crystalline
To Everything a Season – Primavera/Soulstice
Opus 9/11
Symprophecy 2003
Jack
Symprophecy 2004
Being Human Symphony Live
Another Lily for You
The Kenilworth
Clazzy O – Let

2

20

other reasons to kiss a frog

Jonathan Richard Cring

LWS Books
P.O. Box 833
Hendersonville, TN 37077-0833
(800) 643-4718 ext. 74
lwsbooks.com

LWS Books are available at special quantity discounts for
bulk purchases for sales promotions, premiums, fund-
raising, and educational needs. Special books or book
excerpts also can be created to fit specific needs.
For details, write: LWS Books Special Markets,
P.O. Box 833, Hendersonville, TN 37077

ISBN 978-0-9704361-8-4

Library of Congress Control Number: 2005911190

For information on the authors touring schedule visit:
WWW.JANETHAN.COM

Cover Design by Angela Cring, Clazzy Studios

Manufactured and Printed in the United States

Profrogue

To Whom It May Concern:

Actually, I know exactly whom it concerns: all those authors out there who are trying to write the next *how-to* book, possibly by combining existing concepts from previous successes to come up with titles like: ***The Purpose Driven Chicken Soup***, or ***Seven Habits of the Virtuous Women from Venus***.

In the name of God, please stop! And if you happen to be an atheist, then in the name of sense and reason, cease and desist!

Doesn't the very notion of a *how-to* book presume a question that is not in play? In other words WHY!

Therefore I am suggesting that the American publishing field, and, for that matter, the Zimbabwe press, stop manufacturing a deluge of *how-to* books in deference to a new style, a fresh flock of pages, which, for lack of a better term, and also any ingenious quality, I shall dub, *why-to* books.

For, my dear penners of prose and propagators of promises, it is useless to tell someone *how to* do something when you have not yet convinced them that they should even try.

Anyway, *why-to* books open the door to many more avenues of exploration, i.e., *why to work, why to believe, or even why to go on breathing.*

It is my contention that if we give people a reason to aspire, a springboard from which to dive, then we actually might be able to stimulate legitimate interest and therefore unload the glut of *how-to* books that are filling the bins of our bookstores with 75% off stickers.

So if you're looking to put me and my little tome into some sort of genre, you may place us in the self-help or comedy or older children or giddy adult section—under W.T.—for *why-to.* For it was the great philosopher, Amphibious, who said, "At the end of the day, it all boils down to frogs" (even though I would recommend that they are better batter-dipped and fried.)

So, now may I present to you:
Twenty Other Reasons to Kiss a Frog.

Sitting One
They're Green

Yes, frogs are green. Like the grass of the field (unless you happen to live in the commonwealth of Kentucky, where they insist it's blue.) But even in Middlesborough and Louisville, the frogs are green. Who knows, maybe that's where we came up with the phrase "greenbacks" in referring to money. Yes, money and frogs are both green.

But may I note that, although green in color, they are never green with envy. While they may have many questionable habits (for instance, fly consumption and verbal communication that could only be described as a basal burp) frogs really do not desire to be anything else but frogs, not because of a self-righteous superiority, but rather a sense of contentment. "I am green,

I have found my pond, I seek no other sanctuary."

Yes, frogs are green. I know there are those who want to specify the particular shade of green, or even those who would say there is the occasional brown frog, or yellow.

Mutants.

Yes, mutants do exist in our midst, even amongst the kingdom of frogs, but there is something stable and childlike about declaring frogs simply green. Let us be honest. Anyone who is not willing to leave it at that probably has social or emotional problems and it is perhaps better to leave them to their own devices as it pertains to the coloration of a creature tried and true, that we, normal people, possessing no social agenda, know as green.

And may I include that frogs are not green because they're inexperienced, like some recruit stumbling through basic training. No, frogs have been around the block—or at least, the brook. Frogs know they're green, they know the importance of being green and they live in a green world— the forest primeval, where green meets up with brown to form the acceptable muted tones of the garments worn by the average teenager shopping at Abercrombie and Fitch in the month of October.

So what am I saying here? Being green, are frogs fashionable?

Well, I must say that frogs are adaptable. And although they are able to flip over and expose a whitened or yellowed underbelly, they choose to put their best hide forward, which, in this case, is green.

Yes, frogs are green. Isn't it reassuring to know that in this ever-changing world, that somewhere, sitting on a lily pad, is a creature immutable and—green?

Therefore as we begin our series of discussions about the multitude of benefits and blessings granted to us by the frog, let us start with the reality eternal, a truth everlasting: frogs are green. If you come on Wednesday, they will be green. Catch 'em at Christmas—they are also green, although some, in the spirit of the holiday, may don a red bow tie. Catch 'em in springtime: they are green.

Yes, to the frog life is a perpetual 365-day-a-year St. Patrick's celebration. Always the wearing of the green (Notre Dame fans, I would assume, with every croak having the hint of an Irish brogue.)

They embody the great greening of an idea, the notion that new things always have a fresh blossoming color—green with possibilities.

Frogs are green, and you can take that to the bank—along with your greenbacks.

Did I mention Mr. Greenjeans?

Sitting Two
They Have Really Big Eyes

"Grandma, Grandma, what big eyes you have!"

"All the better to see you with, my dear!"

I know this is from the story of Red Riding Hood, and it was about a wolf that was determined to make a young girl his latest snack, but work with me here.

Frogs have really big eyes. Think about it! Their eyes sit up on top of their heads. What a great location—always looking upward—a pair of big peepers gazing to the sky probing for positive potential. You writers of motivational books and anyone who thinks the power of "yes-yes yammer" can do anything at anytime, give heed and please commence to scribble away.

You have found your hero.

Let's review. Frogs have big eyes that sit on the top of their heads, which causes them to look up.

Speaking of eyes and their locations, I am convinced that we evaluate each other by eye angles. Therefore, someone who looks straight ahead? Just keeping their eyes on the road—focused.

Tilt your eyes up a little bit and it's reverence—a pending prayer. If you cast the eyes slightly downward, you get timidity, shyness and the look of some kid you would buy candy from out of pity because you know no one else would ever purchase anything from him.

Eyes further down just a few more degrees to the south and you portray sadness, depression, and a condition that we even call *downcast*.

Yes. The light of the body is the eye. So frogs have an unfair advantage, always seeing what's above their heads—what's flying over—often literally, a fly— SUPPERTIME!

And because the eyes are so large, they seem to be oozing with sincerity. For after all, is there anything more suspicious than a squint? Anything more aggravating than seeing somebody blink their eyes while we are talking to them, visibly showing their lack of interest?

Not the frog! Basically blinkless!

Ponder, if you will. All the money you could save on therapy by simply going to your local lake and sitting down in front of a frog and telling him your problems, knowing that you would have his affixed attention for hours, perhaps days, at a time.

He's the perfect date, sitting quietly, big soulful orbs, looking a little upward... only occasionally croaking out a comment.

Yes, frogs have really big eyes—truly a case of a creature whose eyes are certainly bigger than his belly. Wouldn't we be a better race if our vision were larger than our appetites? Wouldn't we be more intriguing if we were scanning the skies for possibilities?

Frogs have really big eyes, and it's without using any eyeliner.

They're just naturally that way.

Because, after all is said and done, it's not just what we see that produces our outlook, but where we're looking out that determines what we really see.

Frogs have really big eyes, and they don't wear glasses. And they don't have contacts (unless you want to include the occasional dragonfly that squeals when pressured about where to find swarms of flies.)

Sitting Three
They Treat All Women like Princesses

You know the story. The princess goes into the woods, finds a frog, kisses him, and he turns into a prince. Actually, most women will candidly inform you that the process is usually reversed: convincing themselves they have found a prince, they go into the woods, kiss him and end up stuck with a frog.

But, the story (which has to be true, because we tell it to children, and we certainly wouldn't want to mislead our young) tells us something very important.

Frogs must treat all women like princesses. Because after all, you're a frog! How many women are going to kiss you in the first place? At this point are you going to ask for I.D.? Are you going to demand a lineage record to prove her royal highness? Or do you just work under the premise that if she's willing to kiss you, the least you can do is treat her regally? In the mind of a frog (which, honestly, cannot be that expansive—after all we are dealing with a very small cranial area) you work your gig, which has nothing to do with gigging for frogs, which is an entirely different process.

But, as I said, you work your gig! You're a frog. When a woman comes near "bayou" and wants to do a little necking of her own, you go with it. You work it like it's the plan.

You see, frogs don't make the mistake of sitting around and checking on their WEBsite (ha-ha) for the perfect soul mate. Their criteria are simple.

    A. Did she find the woods?
    B. Is she willing to come to my pad?
    C. Can she pucker?
    D. Is she willing to kiss a frog?
    E. Yes, well let's get it on.
    F. She be a princess!

There you have it.

Now, I know there are women out there that would find frogs to be, perhaps, a bit chauvinistic, insisting it's not necessary that women be viewed as princesses, just equals. For you ladies, I would suggest that you avoid frogs. I do offer this warning though: frogs, although certainly not at the top of the looks chain, are stable, having both feet on the ground (if you count water) and are willing to accept you as a lady—just as you are. There are other more handsome species available, but always be aware that many of them are reptilian and certainly most, carnivores.

ATTENTION FEMALES: If you don't want to be treated like a princess, if you don't want the sensation that your kiss is a transforming force, and if you do not want to be part of the miracle of creating a new person filled with confidence through your caress, please (and I must insist) stay away from the frog.

Because frogs treat all women like princesses. Every frog's philosophy is "you never know." Isn't that so true? You just never know. Perhaps each of us should be like the frog—grateful for anyone who would be willing to plant one on our thin, pale, wet lips. But we have much to learn from our green brother.

And let us never forget, frogs are always willing to become princely at just the right moment—as needed—to aid a damsel in distress.

Sitting Four
Most of the Time, They Keep Their Tongues to Themselves

There's nothing worse than an uninvited tongue. Be it in a conversation, in the midst of a kiss, or on today's surprise deli sandwich.

Frogs just know this.

Referring to out last sitting, if you remember the story, when the princess kisses the frog, he does not slip her one.

Have you ever heard of a frog who gossips? Certainly they would be tempted to do so—especially with all those rumors out there about toads. Not to mention the chatter about catfish!

No, frogs keep their tongues to themselves until needed.

And this can't be easy! Sitting inside of their tiny mouth is a sticky tongue that, in some cases, is twice the length of their body! What discipline does it take to hold that thing in there? I'm trying to imagine if I had a twelve-foot tongue! I would be tempted to use it. My God, I would abuse it! I'd be showing it off at parties, bragging, startling unsuspecting lasses.

Yes, frogs have great tongue prowess. But they keep it to themselves! I am sitting here thinking, is there anything that we have as significantly large, wonderful, extravagant and skillful as the frog's tongue that we actually keep to ourselves?

The frog just seems to know why it has a long, sticky tongue. It's for nabbing flies in mid bzzzz. You don't whip the old tongue out for no reason. You don't wag it in gossip about other creatures! You find out early why you've got it, how to use it, and then bring it out at just the right time.

Frogs have really long tongues. But they resist all temptation to wag and brag. Instead they keep it safely curled up inside their own five square inches of space, waiting for the exact right moment to use the great arc of their evolutionary superiority to nab and bring home exactly what they crave.

The tongue may be a mighty member, but none mightier than the frog's. And the human tongue may be unable to be tamed, but not so with our little amphibian neighbor.

Frogs have really long tongues, and they know exactly when to use them. Oh that we, as mere mortals, could learn this single virtue from our mentor!

Yes, nailed on the doorpost of every church, every school and every home in America, should be the byline and credo if you will, of the Kingdom of the Frog:

A little less tongue, please!

Sitting Five
They Eat Pests

Frogs got it figured out.

Anything that buzzes, slithers, squirms—well, dare I need say more—is bad news at Lakeside Commons.

This would include flies worms and snakes. Does anyone like them? And lets be honest—they're not exactly victims of species bias.

They suck (often literally.)

Let's speak of these things.

Flies won't stay out of your business, worms seem to be hygiene challenged and snakes—well, snakes just portray a hostile attitude and will, quite frankly, bite what's closest.

Fortunately for the frog, two out of three of these natural annoyances he just eats. Time has revealed that it is useless to negotiate with a fly or reason with an earthworm.

Best consumed, taken in, digested in small does at leisure.

Now, for the third culprit: the snake. It, of course, is the problem, because snakes, aside from being fussy and persnickety, also happen to have a ravenous appetite for the frog.

Two enemies you can eat and one enemy you must dip and dodge.

The life of the frog.

Digest or divest. (But I digress)

What renders something a pest? A pest is something that takes more than it ever gives. A pest is something that eats, but rarely produces. A pest is something that is needy, but never generous. (So far we're describing everybody's wacky cousin, Wally.)

Did I mention, frogs don't rant and rave about their enemies, nor worry themselves into ulcers about where the next attack is coming from?

Also, frogs don't gossip about flies and worms. I mean what can you say about a fly and a worm that isn't already common knowledge around the water hole?

No, the only path to true pest control is frog logic.

There seems to be some universal application.

What if we, the alleged superior species, took the pests of our lives and consumed what we could and avoided the rest? For instance, if you were a frog, you could go on a rampage amongst your fellow green folk about how annoying flies are and how disgusting worms are, but isn't it just truly better to let these pests expose themselves, allow them to buzz and squirm until all your friends become annoyed enough that they just go ahead and eat them to get them out of the way?

Let's review: worms and flies are not a problem to frogs. They've turned enemies into food.

And snakes are not a problem to frogs because the slitherers telegraph their motions and their intentions so obviously. They wiggle, they slide, they slink and they slather their way up to their prey and then have to open their mouths really big to complete their dastardly attack. Can there be anything more noticeable than a sneaky, slimy pest with a really big mouth?

No, frogs can see snakes coming a mile away. If you think about it, that's why there are more frogs than snakes. Snakes tend to aggravate even the more saintly— just ask Eve. Everybody tries to get them.

Except the frog. He just avoids them and leaves the destroying to other species.

In closing, every creature in all the kingdom of beings must learn how to handle its pests while making sure those aggravations don't end up robbing them of their precious time and energy.

Frogs got it goin'.

They take care of pests.

Without fuss or any need to cuss, they relieve themselves of all their muss.

Sitting Six
Their Pad is a Lily

A great man once said, "Consider the lily."

Frogs do one better. While other folks are out there dallying in the meadow, plucking flowers to discover their inner child, frogs build their home on the lily.

Yes. A lily pad.

What a fabulous innovation! To plant your carcass right on top of a gorgeous, green lily pad, eyes peering out over the splish and splash of a watery domain, yet always in a constant state of flux because lily pads are not stationary.

They're floating.

So even though you have a permanent residence—a lily pad—you are constantly relocating, your home drifting about, similar to a houseboat, or a raft on the Mississippi River with Huck and Tom. (Big Jim also liked frogs)

Frogs don't just consider the lily, they perch on one.

They don't just watch them grow, they grow with them.

Can there be any creature that is more nature-sensitive, more simpatico with its surroundings than the ever-loving frog?

Beavers build dams, snakes slither through the mud. You see, that's the problem with most creatures in our world. They either have to build their own thing, or they settle for the basic surrounding poo and goo. Here's the kicker. The snake wishes he was a beaver and the exhausted beaver pines—"would it be better just to burrow into the mud, like reptile dudes?"

So, no one is ever settled with his or her choice.

Except the frog.

He is of nature, living in nature, existing with nature, and because his home is the lily-pad, dwelling upon nature. . .naturally.

Consider the lily?

No. Make your home there. Then lily life is part of you instead of something you just muse.

Frogs got a lily for a pad.

That's cool.

Sitting Seven
They Fry Up Nicely

Bill saw the sign and thought it was quite curious. Having arrived in town earlier in the afternoon, he grabbed a nap at his local motel, got up, took a shower, put on various forms of smell-good and headed out to his car to—well, to check out the restaurant he had passed earlier and the sign they had out front.

It read: "Tonight, 5-9:00 P.M., our Thursday night delicacy, all the frog's leg's you can eat, $9.99."

Several things struck him about the wording of the sign. Looking at the rustic exterior of the restaurant, the word "delicacy" seemed a little misplaced, especially when referring to something like frog legs. The second thing he found interesting about the sign was the spelling— in particular "frog's leg's." Because, were they offering "frog's legs," or "frog leg's" or "frogs legs," connoting plural frogs with plural legs?

This particular sign offered a fourth option, which was "frog's leg's."

Anyway, were frog legs a delicacy?

He remembered having eaten them once at some place dubbed "The Catfish Something or Other—Barn, Cabin, Castle, Bungalow, Cottage or Shack"—he wasn't sure which one. He had asked the waiter what they tasted like; the young man replied, "Well, they taste like frog."

This was not very helpful to Bill, considering he had never consumed an amphibian before. Pursuing. "Well, what does frog taste like?"

The young server rolled his eyes and said, "Some people think they taste like chicken, but I think that's nuts."

Bill scratched his head. "So you think frogs taste like nuts? Would that be almonds or cashews?"

A second eye roll, a sigh, and the young fellow walked away, disgusted.

Eating frog legs that night, Bill decided they tasted a little like poorly breaded and overly salted chicken breasts.

Nothing worthy of repeat, he thought at the time.

But now, before his eyes, they were being showcased—all you can eat for under ten dollars. He decided to go in and find out what made these particular frog legs so special. Before ordering, he asked the waitress why these frog legs were a delicacy.

"Because they're not leopards," she said.

This was particularly confusing to Bill, because his image of leopards was a large spotted cat from the jungle that was more likely to eat human legs. "Leopard?" Bill inquired.

She smiled. "Yes, we serve only bull-frogs here. Big, fat, juicy bullfrog legs."

It seemed reasonable enough to Bill. What he had probably eaten before were leopards, so no wonder he had been disappointed.

Well, he went to the big buffet and filled up a plateful. He sat down, picked up one of the big frog legs and was about to eat it when he paused. He looked down at his meal and realized that every two legs constituted one frog. A quick count revealed he had seven frogs on his plate, a most disturbing image. It was bizarre. He had never conjured a chicken count at

Kentucky Fried Chicken or a beef depletion at McDonalds.

Seven frogs, he thought to himself. That's an army of frogs.

Bill was quite proud of himself for knowing that more than two frogs was called an army.

Even though a bunch of frogs is called an army, no one has exactly ever felt threatened by them. They've never tried to conquer anyone.

Bill smiled.

An army? More like the horn-tootin Salvation one, he decided.

He sat there staring at his plate filled with his army of frogs, disconcerted. Yes, that would be the word. Somewhere between alarmed and curious, just short of discombobulated.

Disconcerted.

Could he finish his plate of frogs while considering them frogs?

Still, Bill was hungry.

So Bill created a story line.

He projected that these were old frogs that had retired and developed some form of froggy dementia, no longer able to recognize their own pond and families. In an act of mercy, they were gently put to sleep. Then it was discovered that each one of them had signed "Organ Donor" cards requesting that their limbs be donated to the betterment of mankind.

Bill sprouted a tear.

Before him was an army of frogs—veterans of sorts. Brave old fellows who had gone into that long dark night, leaving behind a last wish that they would be consumed and enjoyed by someone. Why not him?

What else could Bill do? How else could he honor the frog brethren, but sink his teeth into their dream and make it his own? He took a big bite.

The brave little green dudes were scrumptious.

He looked down at his plate and said, "God bless you, little froggies. You sure do fry up nicely."

Yes, frogs. They do fry up nicely, leaving behind a great *leg*-acy.

Sitting Eight
They Don't Mind Being Dissected

It takes about twelve hours for a frog to thaw out.

That's what my biology teacher told me. I was twelve at the time.

I don't know why they freeze them—I guess to keep them as fresh as possible.

It was part of my science class, 40% of my six-weeks grade. Each student was given a frog and told to take a little scalpel and dissect him (or her), separate off the parts and, kinda give them a little autopsy.

I don't remember much about the procedure except, for some reason, my frog didn't get totally thawed, so it was very similar to dicing up a slippery moss green Popsicle. I thought it might cut easier if I warmed it, so, this being an era before microwave ovens, I skewered my frog on a pencil and tried to warm him over the Bunsen burner.

And yes, I still do feel stupid, thank you.

Not knowing how long to warm him over the Bunsen burner, in a very few moments, my frog began to stink, alerting everyone that I was toasting frog in the class.

Sufficiently rebuked and rebuffed by my instructor, I was ordered to return to my seat to continue to hack away at my frog.

It was a grodie experience. ("grodie" was a popular word at the time. To ascertain the meaning just imagine the opposite of rad or if bad really meant bad.) Anyway, I did learn through the whole dissection encounter how totally simple this lovely creature really was.

I completed my project. Every time I cut into him, I would apologize for my knifing. (I decided it was a he because the idea of cutting up a girl frog was psycho.)

I do not remember the names of his parts, just that there weren't many and they all looked rather similar.

But the thing that struck me most was that he was not offended.

Maybe his thought was, "I'm done with this body. Go ahead and take it and see if you can get an A, big guy."

Well, I didn't. I mistook some sort of spot of skin for a stomach. But I still was grateful to my friend, the Frog.

It sorta reminded me of when I was a kid, younger. My mother said that when she died she wanted to donate her body to the local college so they could study disease. I thought that was pretty cool. But she got old, her parts broke, she died and nobody remembered what she had said so many years before. They buried her, and nobody ever dissected her and she was never used to cure anything.

Not so with the frog.

When he dies, his lot is pretty well confirmed.

Fried or frozen.

Experiments in high schools or experiments at Maybelline or experiments in a frying pan.

I know some people may think that it's not very meaningful to be dissected by a dumb kid in sophomore biology class, or to give your hide to make sure a new medication isn't lethal, or to fry up nicely for some redneck couple at their engagement party but. . . I will never forget it.

Does anyone ever forget the frog they dissected?

So that means that thousands, maybe millions, of aging Americans in this country have at least one fond memory of the frog.

That's pretty good for a lifetime, don't you think?

For after all is said and done, if you can get one person to remember you fondly, you've done pretty well for yourself.

So here's to you, Fraggy (that's what I named my dismembered frog.)

Thank you for letting me cut you up.

I don't remember why we did it and I don't remember your individual parts.

But as a whole, well, you were A-OK.

Frogs don't object to dissection. For let us be honest. All of us get dissected one way or another.

The frog's lucky enough to wait until he's dead.

Sitting Nine
They Stick To Their Pond

Frogs don't badmouth their home.
They got one up on us there.
Almost everyone has something
negative to say about their hometown,
unless they work for the Chamber of
Commerce, and then they are too obnoxious
to be around others.
I once told a lady I liked her town.
She said,"Well, it's no New York."
That was true. Her town was in
Kansas and New York wouldn't have fit.
Frogs don't badmouth their pond.
Maybe it's because they don't travel much.
Maybe it's because they're easily pleased.
Maybe it's because, from their lily pad,
everything looks pristine, crisp and blue.
Or maybe it's just because they just
work with what they got.
It's time for a story. I own a
swimming pool. One fall we closed up our

pool and the fellow who did the closing did not pull the cover tight enough over the ledge, so, when we uncovered it in the springtime, the pool was filled with various incantations of frogs.

It was like a Darwinian soup.

There were Mama Frogs, Papa frogs, baby frogs, tadpoles, and what looked to be some sort of larval jelly (though not cleared for wheat toast.)

First, I laughed. Well, first I shuddered, but then I laughed. I realized that frogs are willing to work with whatever home you give them. The water was certainly not perfect, being heavily chlorinated and filled with many chemicals.

They just adjusted.

And. . . no complaints. It wasn't like I took the cover off and some frog hopped up and handed me a bill for his medical expenses due to tainted water.

They just raised a family that learned to thrive in chlorine.

Frogs just will not complain about their pond.

I always find it curious when I complain about my hometown when I am a part of the problem by continuing to live there.

Thomas Wolf said, "Can anyone go home?"

You can if you're a frog and you never really left in the first place. Frogs just sit out there on their lily pad thinking to themselves, "This is the best damn water hole in the world."

And maybe, just maybe, because they think it, then it is so.

Because frogs don't have enough brain to pull off "mind over matter." And they don't have enough social grace and training to be courteous.

They're just satisfied.

Satisfied. What a great word. Satisfied—about four degrees cooler than driven and six degrees warmer than complacent.

If you happen to run across a dissatisfied frog, please let me know, because frogs seem to be quite content to live in their own water paradise, even if it's a swimming pool owned by a dumb guy who doesn't know how to put a lid on it. They'll just take advantage of it and call it home.

What a good idea.

Stay satisfied.

Take advantage of it.

Call it home.

Once again, a big thank you to Mr. and Mrs. Frog and all the little tadpoles.

Now, frog family, as to the past due rent for five and a half months, poolside . . .

Sitting Ten
They Ignore Rumors—Warts

Rumors are rampant. Let's just look at a few.

Fat people smell bad.

Black people are dishonest.

Indians are, well, Indian givers.

Spanish people are greasy.

Chinese are cheap.

Germans are Nazis.

English are prisses.

The French are Frogs.

Wait a second! That's not an insult!

But frogs, on the other hand, are not French, but rather, rumored to cause warts.

Even though there has been a great decline in this rumor, and an attempt by some to pass it on to the toad, the vicious innuendo still persists. So, because of it, everyone's a little timid about handling a frog—fear of getting warts.

So what do you do if you're a frog? You can't complain. You can't protest. All you can do is make yourself available for touching, to those brave souls who are willing to take the risk, and then make sure you don't cause any warts.

Because after all, it doesn't do any good to complain about rumors about yourself, and then turn around and fulfill all the stereotypes.

Fat people should make sure they smell good.

Blacks should work hard to maintain an honest report.

Indians should give and not take back.

Chinese should be generous.

Germans—well, Germans should not be Nazis.

English should work hard at maintaining a sufficient amount of machismo.

And French—well, I guess French could stay frogs. (Quite an honor, actually.) It's just real hard to stop a rumor when you're helping to maintain the veracity of it. For after all, it may not be prejudice if people can prove you are what they claim.

Frogs don't sweat the small stuff.
(Matter of fact, frogs don't really sweat.
They just get oily.)

Frogs don't protest.

Frogs don't procure civil rights.

Frogs just make themselves available to be touched and make sure that they don't fulfill the rumors about warts.

There is a wonderful three-step procedure to overcoming rumors:

1. Ignore them the best you can.
2. Counteract them by being the opposite of what's been said.
3. Never pass a rumor along to anyone else about anything else.

Pretty soon, rumors won't carry any weight any more. Just somebody's opinion. And you know what they say about opinions. Opinions are like toads—have too many of them and pass them along and you'll get warts.

Well, that's what I've heard.

Sitting Eleven
They Jump At Opportunities

I was trying to remember the last time I jumped. I guess I was a lot younger, playing basketball, trying to get a rebound, although the coach insisted that he rarely saw daylight under my feet.

There is much to be said for jumping. What is the saying—"fools jump in where angels fear to tread?" Something like that. You know what the trouble is with a lot of those old sayings. They were written by old men and old women. Old people who had forgotten what it was like to be young and spry and ready to go.

Frogs jump. I never did understand that *Twelve Days of Christmas* song. What is it, "Ten Lords a Leaping?" Well, I never saw a leaping lord. When I think of leaping, I think of frogs. Frogs jump. Mark Twain wrote a story about it. Matter of fact, I think they still have some sort of frog jumping contest out in Calaveras County. 'Cause frogs jump.

Sure enough, sometimes you gotta poke them with a stick to get them to move, but if you jab them, their first instinct is to jump. If you probe me, I manage some kind of movement, but I never muster a jump.

Frogs jump at the opportunity to move. Yes, there's much to be said for enthusiasm. Enthusiasm covers a multitude of talentlessness.

I believe I would much rather have an enthusiastic person working for me than a lazy know-it-all. And one of the reasons for that is that people who jump are infectious. I watched a frog jump just the other day, and it was so impressive that it made me want to get up, move around, and hop about.

You never see a committee of frogs discussing whether they should do something. They just perch on their lily pad to think about it, and then they jump.

It seems we live in a generation that has learned how to be depressed even before anything bad ever happens. I overheard a woman talking to a friend. It went something like this: "Yes, I got to go to the mall." (Sigh.) "Gotta buy myself a new pair of shoes." (Still another sigh.) "And then go pick up my dry cleaning." (This time, just a lift of shoulder, with no sigh.) "And then go out to lunch at the ladies club." (Still a deeper sigh.) "And then I better get some gas in the car." (A shake of the head.) "And then I gotta go home and pay some bills." (The deepest sigh of all.)

You would have thought the woman was on death row, when actually what she just described was getting a new pair of shoes, getting freshly cleaned clothes, a delicious lunch, a full tank of gas, while possessing enough money to pay her bills! I know some people would say it's just how you look at it, but have you ever wondered if reality is more about how life looks at us and our joy in the tasks, instead of how we look at life and the painfulness of responsibility?

Frogs got it figured out. If you have to move, you might as well jump. Go ahead and jump! (I hope I don't owe Van Halen a royalty.) Yes, frogs jump at opportunity. Actually frogs jump whenever they're prodded to do so. And sometimes they just do it for the sheer fun of it. And, my dear friend the frog, I'm going to check into that *Twelve Days of Christmas* thing and see if I can't get *you* leaping in there instead of them lords.

Sitting Twelve
They Aren't Ashamed They Started As Tadpoles

A dear friend of mine insists that she birthed a pretty baby. She shows me pictures. I'm fairly tolerant, but I must be honest with you and tell you that this child is one of the ugliest formations of baby flesh I've ever seen in my life. I don't know how to tell her directly that she spawned a mess. I do joke with her about it and point out certain idiosyncrasies in the mass of ugliness. But this is one horrible misuse of baby skin.

Most of us, though, are fairly proud of our baby pictures—both ours and our offspring's. But we do reach a certain age where everybody's a little uncomfortable about how they look. I just don't see a whole lot of people plopping down pictures of themselves between the years of six and fifteen. It's kind of like pulling an apple pie out of the oven thirty minutes too soon. You look at it and get the general idea of where it may be heading, but right now it's an uncooked, doughy mess.

That's the way most of us look in our tadpole era. Because tadpoles don't look like frogs. Tadpoles have tails and frogs don't. Frogs have heads, and tadpoles try real hard, but nothing's quite formed there. Most of our formative years look quite deformed.

Frogs are not ashamed of their beginnings. They understand that they started out as tadpoles. And tadpoles are just damn ugly.

Tadpoles look like overgrown sperm. They swim like them. And they're just kind of gross. But somewhere deep in the heart of every tadpole is the knowledge that someday, it will join the regal ranks of its righteous renderers—the frog. And deep in the memory of every frog is the fact that it was once a slithering, slimy, wiggling, nondescript tadpole. And this was just a necessary step in completing and achieving frogdom.

There is a wonderful, wonderful phrase that says, "Do not despise small beginnings." Often knowing where we came from grants us insight about where we should go. Frogs were tadpoles. Of course,

48

if frogs had stayed tadpoles, they would have had a severe public relations problem. But they don't. Just like we don't stay awkward, gangling, stumbling twelve-year-olds all of our lives (unless we desire to do so.)

We'll get there. We'll become full-fledged adults. And it's our job to not be ashamed of our tadpole years. Because frogs sure remember when they were tadpoles, and were more the tail than the head.

But frogs are pretty smart. No one's born a frog. You're born tadpole. Swim along, enjoy it, do the best you can. But some day you'll be a frog, raising some tadpoles of your own and it's important you remember what it was like to be one. Because it's essential that you not be ashamed of your tadpole years and therefore critical of the tadpoles you've spawned.

No, frogs are not ashamed of having been tadpoles. Matter of fact, it's one of the standing jokes in the pond: How many tadpoles does it take to catch a fly? Answer: Tadpoles don't catch flies. You have to wait a week until they become a frog.

As you can see, it's not real funny unless you live on a lily pad.

Sitting Thirteen
They Are Amphibians—All Wet, All Dry, Who Cares?

Are amphibians, perhaps, the only evidence existing today that we all may actually have come from each other?

You know.

Evolution.

Without amphibians, you'd have reptiles and birds and elephants and monkeys and humans, but it's this little creature—I guess normally little—the amphibian, that's wedged somewhere between reptile, fish and badger, that demonstrates to us that somebody somewhere was determined to put together a design.

Fish live in water and reptiles normally on land. (Although they do bathe occasionally.) But amphibians have a little bit of fish in them and a little bit of snake and a little bit of muskrat. (Well I have exhausted my scientific insight.)

Frogs.

A creature for all seasons, all climates, all temperatures. Put it on land, it'll hop along. Put it in the water, it'll take its great big feet and swim. It just doesn't care. While a fair percentage of the creatures on the planet Earth pursue a utopian locale, frogs just blend in to their surroundings and become part of whatever they're on or in.

Put them on land, they're a land creature. Put them in water, they're a water creature. Put them on a plate, they're a meal. (I apologize for that tasty aside.)

All wet, all dry. Makes no difference. They maintain their identity. They are amphibians, linked to all of creation by various body parts that resemble everyone.

God, isn't that wonderful? The body of a fish, the skin of a snake, the feet of a duck, the hind legs of a lizard.

Frogs. A salute to the animal kingdom, tipping their hats, as it were, to every living creature. Wet or dry, they remain in the mix.

Frogs don't seem to mind. They adjust their body temperature to where they are. They blend into the surroundings; they go with the go and flow with the flow.

Frogs aren't picky. Is there any nicer thing you can say about a creature?

"They're not picky."

Because even though most of us excuse pickiness in ourselves by dubbing it personal choice, in others?

Fussy, arbitrary, intolerant, inflexible, and, may I add at this point, anti-frog?

Non-frog.

Frogus non-gratis.

Because, honest to God, we live in a non- frog world, where personal taste is revered over personal sense, where choice is more important than reason and opinion supersedes history.

I, for one, am weary of living in a non-frog world. I'm proud to be of the human species and equally proud to be an American. But I would like to acquire a third citizenship. I'm asking if those noble amphibians, the frogs, would accept me as an honorary member, so that I, too, wet or dry, land or sea, day or night, cold or hot, might learn to adapt, adjust and succeed swimmingly.

As of the writing of this book, I am still waiting for a reply from the frog court of records to see if my application has been accepted.

Will they have me as a member of their army? I am hoping and we shall see. Perhaps you would like to join, too. There is something wonderful about being a frog—an amphibian—a blending of all creation, a part of each, a segment of the whole, yet unique unto you.

Jonathan Richard Frog. I sniff a classic.

Sitting Fourteen
You Know What They Say About Big Feet

Frogs are never insecure about where they stand with others. (or, in their case, crouch.)

Does anyone have an in-between opinion on frogs?

Icky or adorable.

I mean, have you ever heard anybody go, "Oh, yeah, frogs. They're all right."

After all, indifference is the common malady causing all creatures to scramble for a brief moment's attention.

Anyway (without the benefit of segue) frogs have big feet. Unnaturally large feet. There is a young wives fable that big feet are —well, you know—a sign of big everything.

I know not.

And, I'm sure I'm getting my measurements incorrect here, but proportionally, if my feet were as large as a frog's, in relation to my body, I would wear a size 89 shoe—89 Triple EEE.

Not particularly attractive.

You would have folks constantly making cracks:

"Here he comes! Something must be afoot!"

Or

"With feet like that, he must be quite a sole singer…"

still pursuing it,

"His feet are so big he could toe my car…"

These are un-funny, off the cuff remarks made by annoying people who punctuate the horrible humor with their own laughter while slapping your back—you grimace.

Frogs have really big feet.

They just use them.

What a great idea! If each and every one of us would use the physical attributes we have to our advantage, why would we ever need approval?

Oh, but not us.

We are constantly messing with our "head to toe," pursuing our perfect persona.

Not frogs. Let's look at it. Frogs have a big throat, but they don't go in to get a throat tuck. They have big feet, but they don't go to get their webs cropped. Black freckles. Come on! What could be worse than black freckles? But, no skin creams on a frog's nightstand.

They work with it.

Meanwhile back at the human pond: No one seems to be satisfied with the people package proffered. Why? Because there are only three or four "looks" in vogue in the male of our species and three or four in the female. So everyone tries to squeeze (good word) into these molds and settle within the borders of the Kingdom of Beauty with its capital—Adequacy.

We're boring.

I return.

Frogs have really big feet. We might assume it's because they need them. But I say it's because they use them, and therefore it appears they need them. If we would just take our physical attributes, those not threatening our health, and use them to our advantage, all our quirks would soon be just US—accepted.

If black, fat, Korean, Portuguese, skinny, German, gay, Republican, liberal, lactose intolerant, tattooed, relish or mustard, stylist or Super Cuts, NFL or college football, medium rare or well done, and. . . Mormons would start walking relaxed about who they are and acting as if it's normal instead of aspiring to some level of immediate inclusion, it would just be assumed that's who they are, and who they were born to be.

Tick-tock. Time passes.

Frogs have big feet. Sorry ladies, I don't think they have a whole lot of other big things. But they have big feet. So they use them.

What an idea! I got something different—instead of changing it, I use it.

In conclusion: frogs think really well on (and about) their feet.

Sitting Fifteen
Their Front Legs Don't Have Back Leg Envy

I was once asked to be a judge at a beauty contest. Don't get the wrong idea— it wasn't Miss America. I don't remember right now what the title was. Miss Hogwash Hollow, or something like that. I do remember this young lady walking on the stage. She was stunning. She had all the characteristics normally associated with typical American beauty. She was about five foot nine, brunette, well-proportioned, slender but not too skinny, perfect skin, straight teeth.

She stood—a statuesque pose. My job was to ask her a question. The question was, "What is the first thing you would do to try to relieve the poverty in our world?"

She stood for a moment, contemplating. And then she spoke. Honestly, I do not remember her answer, because her voice was the most comical blending of nasal screech and cornpone that I had ever heard. I released an involuntary chuckle which I quickly stifled. I failed to hear her answer because I was too busy thinking to myself, "Yep. God got her."

Let's be honest—nobody has it all. God balances blessing with blasting. A little good—a little bad. Someone with talent often suffers from other drawbacks. Someone with a perfect body often fails to deliver an equivalent personality.

It's the same thing with the frog. Frogs have two gloriously long back legs. And two little tiny stubs up front. But they are never tempted to get their body parts mad at each other. Yes, I think that's what we do. We get our nose mad at our ears because they're not proportional. We get our thighs mad at our butt because they're competing for the least cellulite. We get our lips mad at our hair because the colorations aren't just right. Unlike the frog, we create a warring in our own members for no particular damn good reason.

Frogs got it figured out. You got two long legs and two short legs per customer. And when you think about it, how ridiculous would four long legs be? Does the word "awkward" come to mind? And four short legs? No hopping. Just stumbling.

The design is always right on the mark to propel the package.

Frogs have two legs for jumping and two legs for stopping.

Symmetry.

If we just knew that, we wouldn't be constantly trying to create something that is against the natural order.

Frogs don't suffer from back leg envy. The front legs do what the front legs do. And the back legs do the rest. What a great idea! Frogs don't ask their front legs to be back legs. They don't look at their front legs as shortcomings, nor do they ask their back legs to trim. You work with the design, you accept the design, or you spend your whole life trying to change the design.

Not a frog. They only have four or five years. Should they spend six months of it stressing?

Maybe that was God's failure with human life span. He actually ended up giving us too many years. So we feel we have time to screw around constantly reinventing ourselves.

Stop reinventing yourself. Find your formula, patent it and go peddle it in the marketplace.

Frogs don't war within their members. The back legs are always very complementary of the front ones. What a great word. Spelled *complimentary*, it means to praise. Spelled *complementary*, it means to support. Isn't that what we crave as people? Some praise, some support.

Frogs don't have leg envy. They work with what they possess. And because they do, what they've got works.

Sitting Sixteen
They Are Strongly Against Pollution

I had a nightmare that a nine-foot frog ducked through the doorway of my home, came in and squatted on my dining room table, threw up on my couch, broke my bed and left, laughing. I think I remember he was also wearing a backpack.

I think it's safe to assume that most of us would be offended by such an event; dare I say, alarmed? But if you're a frog, this happens practically every day of your life. Some big, hulking human comes to your pond or your wooded area and dumps all his trash, waste products and chemical run-offs in the middle of your living room, flowing right by your lily-pad.

What are you gonna do?

Like, in my case, what are you going to say to a nine-foot frog? It's pretty doggone intimidating (not to mention you don't know what he's got in his backpack.)

Let's put this into historical perspective. Human beings have always pummeled the planet. Whenever it is in our power to overtake a smaller fellow and establish our will, we do it and hope in the long run that it works out to mutual advantage. Violence is violent. It isn't all right because things seem all right. It is wrong.

The United States promotes its greatness, yet, without the sacrifice and forgiveness of the Native and African Americans, the thankless labor of the abolitionists and the work ethic of a human flood of ethnic groups who were once alienated and persecuted, we would still be a floundering group of colonies trying to agree on an acceptable tax for tea.

Yet, we continue to persist in the persecutions of our day. When's the last time a frog kicked your ass? He should.

Even though we pollute his home and destroy his environment, he quietly adapts, taking on a monk-like simplicity of mercy and fortitude mingled with foresight and innovation in the presence of less-than-ideal circumstances.

Frogs don't like pollution. Believe me, they would tell you if they could. And hopefully, we won't send any chemicals or radioactive material into their pond that will cause them to grow to nine feet. Because if we do, don't be surprised if they hop into your home and crash your little world.

By the way, if one does, would you find out what's in his backpack?

Sitting Seventeen
They Don't Like Snakes

Most of us don't like what we used to
be. Otherwise, we'd still be that, right?

Frogs are related to snakes
somewhere along the line. But frogs have
outgrown being snakes.

Snakes hiss.

Frogs ribbbet.

Snakes slither.

Frogs hop.

Snakes bite.

Frogs, well—don't.

If you're a frog, you certainly don't
want to be bigoted against the snake, yet,
you don't want to be a snake again. And
when the invitations arrive for the Reptile
Reunion, well, you just make other plans.

Frogs look at it this way: we are
snakes who have gotten over our social
problems.

Is there anything good about the snake? The snake is the symbol of temptation and evil. The snake is poisonous. The snake rattles. The snake has a forked tongue (which any good Apache will tell you, is bad news.) The snake is scaly. The snake sheds its skin but really doesn't change. Is it all right if frogs ignore the snake without everyone feeling that they hate them?

Frogs just don't like snakes.
Don't:
    a. wish to be snakes.
    b. admire snakes.
    c. And most of all, don't wish to socially interact with them.

Snakes think things are fun that frogs find unacceptable. First of all, snakes are gullible. And where do frogs get that idea? Snakes swallow things whole.

Frogs don't. Frogs take things in and digest them, slowly.

Frogs just don't like snakes. They understand it's a part of their roots, they accept it was part of frog emergence.

But doesn't the word emergence mean that we've emerged? We've outgrown that phase?

They never say "We're only frogs."
But I have heard a
frog say, "I must apologize. That was a
little bit of the snake in me."

Frogs have learned to accept that
some of their heritage has left a dark cloud
over their history. Apologies. But the best
way to express an apology is by becoming
better frogs.

So, in conclusion, frogs wish to
inform us that, although they don't like
snakes, they don't really think about snakes
that much, because they are too busy
becoming the best frogs they can be.

If a frog was here, he would probably
say—"Please forgive the snake in all of us,
and accept that we are new creatures—frogs.
And may we grow and be stronger in our
frog image every day."

{And, while we are at it, please
forgive the "white man" in me that has
caused the subjugation of people with
difference and color over the centuries.}

Sitting Eighteen
Humans Are A Problem

So what do you do with someone who wants to pee in your stream and chop your legs off and eat them?

Thus the frog's dilemma with humans.

I have been asked, because of writing this book, and doing research and spending a little time lakeside with a couple of frog buddies, to offer the following letter from the organization, ***Frogs Are People, Too—Kinda***.

Dear All Human Types,

Hi, how are you doing? Hope things are going well. I hear rumors of good—and bad. But honestly, not that affected by most of it. I see you standing on the shoreline with your poles and lines in the water, trying to catch fish, drinking out of large brown bottles, yelling and playing loud music. We really don't have much problem with that. After all, everybody's got to eat, and we certainly don't let a swarm of flies pass us by without taking our fair share.

It's just that, while you're out there, enjoying the day, could you keep in mind that you're big and powerful? I don't know whether you know it or not, but bred inside each and every frog is a deep respect for your species. We think you're kind of cool. Your design is a little unusual, but still not gross.

We don't have much to complain about, except that, with power and with authority comes responsibility. We really don't mind moving over and making room for you. We were just wondering whether or not you could make room for us, too?

Can we offer an insight? I don't know whether you can continue to become successful as a species when you look at every other creature as either food or a pest. With all due respect, is it possible for you to consider us as fellow occupants of a common planet—friendly tenants in a well-managed apartment complex?

We really don't want your turf. I mean, you can have the cities and the towns and the villages and the cars and the roads.

Honestly, you can have almost all of it. If you could just leave us the lakes, the ponds and the forests. Honest to God, we could make do.

And then you could come out and visit us. And we would be so glad to see you, because the surroundings would be clean and our home replenished and ready. I know you're not used to listening to frogs, but we thought maybe this one time you might be open to hearing from us and consider us as your comrades. For, isn't it incredible, no, magnificent, that we happen to be sharing this Earth at the same time?

Because in frog world, we contend that what goes around comes around. And you may not think that we're very important, but if we go extinct, what's to say you're not next?

We don't want to have hard feelings toward you humans. We would just like you to be better caretakers of the planet. You seem to be the ones in charge right now. My ancestors had to deal with the dinosaurs, which really didn't give a damn about any other creatures, just looked on them as food and pests.

Well, the dinosaurs are gone. A word to the wise, you know.

So we will be seeing you. And we look forward to sharing with you. And we hope you will take this letter in the spirit it was given.

We really would like to like you.

Sincerely,

Your friend, the frog

Sitting Nineteen
They're Name-Challenged, But...

"A rose by any other name would be just as sweet."

Baloney.

Are you trying to tell me if a rose were called a gork, that men would gladly send a dozen long-stemmed gorks to their girlfriends? After all, what rhymes with gork? What would it be, a gork for my dork?

No.

Names do make a difference.

That's why we take weeks, sometimes months, painstakingly naming our children, knowing that this handle will be stuck on them their whole life. So even though Ulysses sounds really good at four o'clock in the morning, on birthing day we opt for Brian.

Well, so far, we have avoided the subject. Let's be honest. Frogs are name-challenged. Frogs is not really a name—more a sound young boys repeat to make young girls giggle. Yet, perhaps there is more to the explanation. Is it because of the name or because of the way frogs look, or because the only communication they possess is to croak?

Who knows?

But, at the very least, it seems, the name frog invokes a smirk.

For years this bothered the frog. No one wants to be disrespected for their name.

Take the name "tiger." It's become a mascot for sports teams all over the world. Is there a sports team that is called the Frogs? They even have the Mighty Ducks. But aside from Texas Christian University (TCU), which calls itself the Horned Frogs, feeling the need to add the frightening addition of horns, no team would dare to call itself by the name of this beloved, yet name impaired, amphibian.

Understand this, other names have been considered.

One frog suggested "Webbers." But it sounded a little too much like a dot.com company, and God knows what's happening to them on the market.

Another frog suggested "Greenaters." But it was quickly. pointed out that it resembled the old TV show, *Green Acres.*

Another frog suggested, "Tongue Masters." But it was generally agreed that it sounded a bit too Kung Fu.

One name that was almost adopted was "Amphibs." But—when the word spread other creatures began to literally come out of the woodwork, objecting to the frogs taking on the entire scope of the amphibian genus.

They always returned to frogs. And you know, it never will get better. It just is what it is. And the frog, having learned to accept his feet, his back legs as meat, his elongated sticky tongue and rumors about his penchant to cause warts, has once again made an adaptation—to absorb his name.

So, frogs it is.

(Too bad Granddaddy Longlegs is taken.)

{Oh, and by the way, our name-challenged friends, the frogs, would really like us to stop saying "we have a frog in our throats." That's really gross.}

Sitting Twenty
They Tolerate Kermit

It's downright embarrassing.
Children's Workshop may think it's funny.
Or cuddly. But around the pond it's totally
humiliating. You know what we're talking
about.
    Kermit.
    Kermit…the frog. Or so they say.

    Did anyone notice? Kermit walks
erect. When's the last time you saw a frog
standing on its hind legs? It was a
nightmare, right?
    Not done.
    Not cool.
    Let's talk about Kermit's voice.
Anyone recently run across a frog that is a
tenor? Kermit has a voice like somebody's
holding his nose and squeezing his middle
all at the same time.
    Not basal.
    Not an appropriate croak.

And certainly doesn't have a rumbling roll of a ribbbet.

Of course, the worst injustice of all. What self-respecting frog would be caught dead dating a pig? It's disrespectful to the sisters! What, the frogs in the hood aren't good enough? You have to go to the barnyard and start dating some blonde-haired porker? And if they wed--what would the offspring look like? Who wants to see a pig with long legs and a four-foot tongue?

Are you frightened yet?

How would you feel, as human beings, if somebody came down to the planet and picked, well, let's say, picked Pee-Wee Herman, to represent your species around the whole galaxy? I think we would hear a few complaints from parlors and pantries.

And then...Kermit sings that song, "It's Not Easy Being Green."

What color would you like, Kermie?

Green is one of our best attributes. (Please refer to Sitting One.)

But, with all the grumbling that occurs around the pond (and, believe me, there's plenty of it) the consensus amongst the frog population is to let it go.

Yes, frogs tolerate Kermit.

Because, as uncomfortable as they are with some of the images presented, especially with impressionable young children, at least they're being included and talked about. And what's the old saying? There's no such thing as bad publicity. And if people are talking about you, you must be doing something right. Still, keep in mind that no self-respecting frog would be caught dating a pig.

If you have some time, go to your local pond and get to know a real frog. You will find that he's quite different from Kermit. He's green and proud of it. He's adaptable and just won't quit. And he's forgiving—even if you pollute his streams and name a stuffed puppet after him. He'll just give a smile and look at you with his big eyes, and say, "Ribbbetus, ribb--ribbcroak." Which loosely translated from Frog, means, "Give me a kiss and watch what happens?"

So there you have it—20 OTHER REASONS TO KISS A FROG. Oh, I am sure men better than myself could come up with 50.

But twenty is a good start.

Just take a moment to imagine our world as a great theater occupied with all variety of entities and creatures. Yes, a theater. Sometimes you are backstage eating off the deli tray. Sometimes in the wings waiting for your entrance. Sometimes it's on stage doing dialogue and every once in awhile, it is your soliloquy to a hushed house. We all take our turn, both with our name in lights and with pushing the broom to clean the floor of ticker tape from a parade—one in which we were not even invited.

So put on your make-up, don your favorite costume, learn your lines, and respect your fellow actors—even the green ones.

And then.

Wait for your cue and go out there and "Break a leg."

(My apology to the frogs—sensitive area!)

Jonathan Richard Cring

Jonathan Richard Cring is the composer of ten symphonies, the author of seven books, including **I'M . . . the legend of the son of man, Liary, Holy Peace . . .the story of Iz and Pal, Jesonian, Finding the Lily and Digging for Gold.** His thirty-year experience has taken him from the grease paint of theater to a time as an evangelist among the gospel saints. He is the winner of a Billboard Music Award and is the in-house composer for the Sumner County Symphony. He travels the country lecturing as an advocate for the Jesonian movement. He has been married for thirty-four years and is the father of three sons and guardian to three others. He lives in Hendersonville, Tennessee.

Also from the Author

All books available through Amazon.com and
WWW.LWSBOOKS.COM

Jesonian
A decision to take spirituality personally.
ISBN 978-0-9704361-4-6

Stagnancy is the decision to settle for less than we know we need. In every generation there must be a voice reminding us of our true mission, prodding us on to escape mediocrity and stirring the waters to freshen the stream of thinking. Jesonian is a book that poses the questions in the heart of every human who seeks to find some nourishment for his hardening soul – every man, woman and child who yearns for a message with meaning and wants to escape the rigors of religion and find the true spirit in spirituality.

Finding the Lily (to consider)
A journette of the journey.
ISBN 978-0-9704361-5-3

When I was a kid, they didn't have Big Men's Stores - at least, none my parents told me about. So my mother would buy me the only pants she could find in my size - work pants.

Also from Jonathan Richard Cring

Dickie work pants. For some reason, she would choose the green ones - the color created by smashing a bag of green peas into a frog. And speaking of being smashed, for some reason, she wouldn't buy them my size, I guess because she didn't want to admit how big I was. And so she would purchase them so small that I would have to suck in to button them. That's what you like when you're fat. Tight green clothes. Of course, these pants were so stiff they could stand by themselves, which I have to admit, came in handy when waiting in line at an amusement park.

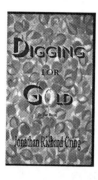

Digging for Gold [in the rule]
ISBN 978-0-9704361-6-0

The Golden Rule, Do unto others as you would have them do unto you, loses some of its gleam and luster when merely decoupaged and hung on a wall in a Sunday School class as some sort of insipid platitude, more an aspiration than a lifestyle.

In DIGGING FOR GOLD (in the rule), author Cring examines the intricacies and passion of the original thought and also offers innovative approaches to turning the "Rule" into a reality.

Chocked full of stories, examples and plans of action, DIGGING is a must for the soul who desires to have their spirituality flowing in the mainstream instead of entombed in the sanctuary of religious redundancy.

Also from Jonathan Richard Cring

Holy Peace . . . the story of Iz and Pal
ISBN 978-0-9704361-3-9
In a basket full of oranges, it is always the singular apple that gains our attention. This is a wonderful characteristic of the human soul. So in our day and age, in the midst of clamoring for resolutions based on military might, a breath of fresh air comes in to the atmosphere of pending war. Amir and Jubal – two boys who grew up on different sides of the tracks of a conflict – one Arab, one Jew. They rename themselves Iz and Pal and determine to maintain their friendship amidst the granite – headed thinking of their friendship amidst the granite-headed thinking of their society. Where their journey takes them, the friends they make along the way, the surprising enemies, and the stunning resolution, will keep you riveted to the brief pages of this odyssey into peace.

I'M . . . the legend of the son of man
ISBN 978-0-9704361-3-9
A novel on the life of Jesus Christ focusing on his humanity, passion, and personality—highlighting struggles with his family, sexuality, abduction by zealots, humor and wit, and interaction with characters bound by tradition, affection, legalism, politics, and religious

Also from Jonathan Richard Cring

fanaticism—congealed into a 416 page entertaining and inspirational quick read; non-theological and mind enriching.

Preparing a Place [for myself]
ISBN 978-0-9704361-7-7

The perfect book for all those folks who would like to die just long enough to find out what the crap is going on – then come back to pizza. I always wanted to meet God. When I was a child, very small, I thought he would look like Reverend Bacorra, a Presbyterian minister I knew- salt and pepper hair, tall, glasses, donning a black robe, wearing oxblood, shiny shoes with scuffed tips.

As I grew older my image changed, but always, I envisioned a physical presence – an actual being. Now, where was God?

I wondered if God was merely light, love and spirit. I smiled at my own ramblings. Light, love and spirit - not a bad triangle.

Still, I wanted to meet God, fact to face, as it were.
a bad triangle.
Still, I wanted to meet God, fact to face, as it were.

Mr. Kringle's Tales . . .
26 stories 'til Christmas
ISBN 978-0-9704361-1-5

Twenty-six great Christmas stories for young and old An advent calendar of stories ranging from the hilarious "Gunfight at the Okay Chorale" to the spine-chilling "Mr. Kringle Visits the President", to the futuristic "Daviatha".

Ask for these titles at and all titles from **LWS Books** at:

• Your local bookstore

• WWW.LWSBOOKS.COM

• WWW.AMAZON.COM